The World I See

By Erica Vargas

Illustrated by Cara Dunning

To my cousin Tootsie:

Thank you for your constant support and for seeing the beauty in my story.

Love, Erica

Published by E-Logic Productions
©2021 Erica Vargas DBA E-Logic Productions

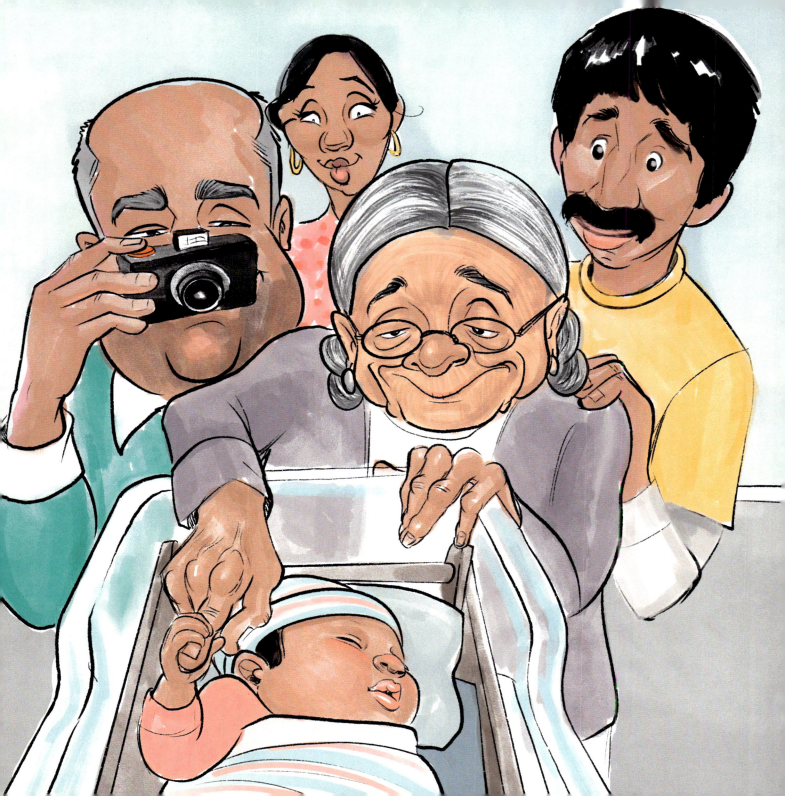

The smell of the ocean and taste of salt water, kelp surrounding my feet.
On my back the sun gets hot but I love the heat.

"We're at the top", my father says as we sit to rest our feet.
After all the work to climb up here, this is quite a treat.

It is so neat to feel beneath me all the extra space, and listen as the clouds below move at a different pace.

So freely they run, neighing as their hooves hit the ground, they jump and prance and dart like no one is around.

The baby foal is drinking from it's mother's udder,
getting the food it can not get from any other.
The sway of the grass, the leaves rustling to and fro.
The peace, calm and sunshine make you never want to go.

There is always a lot to do when we're at Aunt Suzy's farm, and so I like to visit to witness all it's charm.

The pigs in their pen with their hair real rough and noses wet with water;

I laugh when they eat so fast they slurp and slurp and slobber.

The power of it's crashing water;
the wind blows my hat away.
We all have on our raincoats which we
almost left at home that day.

It's so forceful and exciting you want to jump around,
but I held tight onto the rails for fear of falling down.

I imagine that it is like a tidal-wave would surely sound,
hearing the splash and crash of water all around.

The sounds were never ending,
people talking in the air,
live music in the park and
smell of great food everywhere.

The hard stone feeling goes forever underneath my feet,
I race around with brother and I never cheat.
I could hear and feel the people walking long and far,
and when my brother passed me, he felt like such a star.

It was so long that I was sure it would never end,
and just as I thought it was over, there was another bend.

The trees are so big and strong
that they can carry me,
but I can't even hug around them
because their too wide you see.

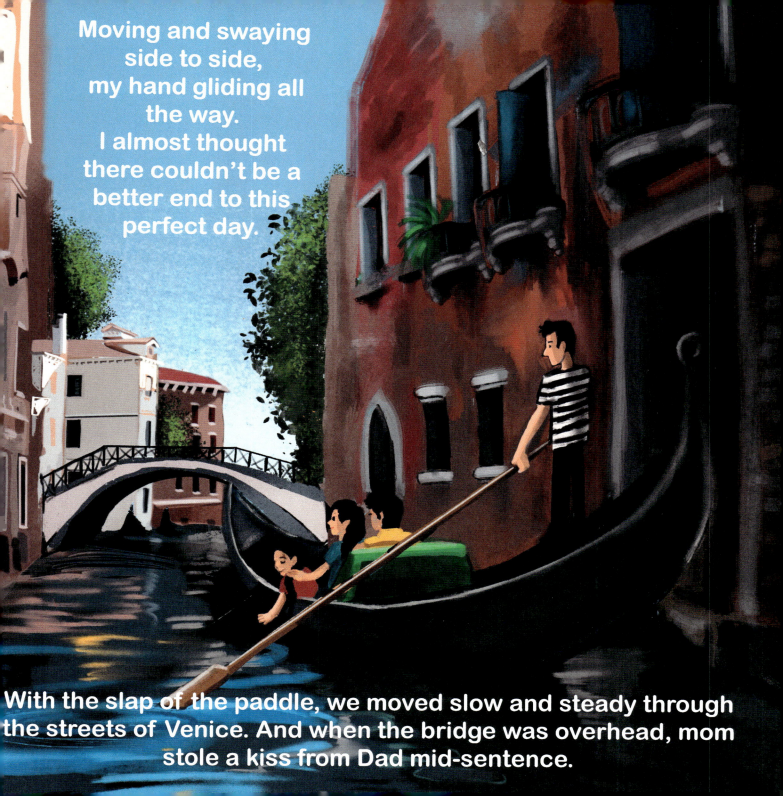

Moving and swaying side to side,
my hand gliding all the way.
I almost thought there couldn't be a better end to this perfect day.

With the slap of the paddle, we moved slow and steady through the streets of Venice. And when the bridge was overhead, mom stole a kiss from Dad mid-sentence.

Winding down to go to sleep
what adventures I have each day.
Because, I am SEEING the world all
around me, in my very own special way.

The End

ABOUT THE AUTHOR

Erica was born and raised in Los Angeles, California. She was always an adventurous child and enjoyed gathering new experiences. From an early age she loved telling stories and acting out skits to her friends and Family - a natural story teller. She now resides in Florida with her husband and son

ABOUT THE ILLUSTRATOR

Cara Dunning is an illustrator currently based in Nashville, TN. She worked as a caricature artist at Walt Disney World in Florida for 13 years and attended the University of South Florida at Tampa, where she studied painting and printmaking. When she isn't working on illustrations she is writing and performing her original music. She loves bringing stories to life and figuring out how to best communicate their beauty.

Made in the USA
Coppell, TX
30 May 2021